EPIC BOOKS are no ordinary books. They burst with intense action, high-speed heroics, and shadows of the unknown. Are you ready for an Epic adventure?

This edition first published in 2023 by Bellwether Media, Inc.

No part of this publication may be reproduced in whole or in part without written permission of the publisher. For information regarding permission, write to Bellwether Media, Inc., Attention: Permissions Department, 6012 Blue Circle Drive, Minnetonka, MN 55343.

Library of Congress Cataloging-in-Publication Data

LC record for Ferrari F8 Tributo available at: https://lccn.loc.gov/2022020228

Text copyright © 2023 by Bellwether Media, Inc. EPIC and associated logos are trademarks and/or registered trademarks of Bellwether Media, Inc.

Editor: Kieran Downs   Designer: Jeffrey Kollock

Printed in the United States of America, North Mankato, MN

TABLE OF CONTENTS

ONE SMOOTH RIDE	4
ALL ABOUT THE F8 TRIBUTO	6
PARTS OF THE F8 TRIBUTO	12
THE F8 TRIBUTO'S FUTURE	20
GLOSSARY	22
TO LEARN MORE	23
INDEX	24

ONE SMOOTH RIDE »

A Ferrari F8 Tributo blasts down a road. The driver hits the gas. The car roars ahead.

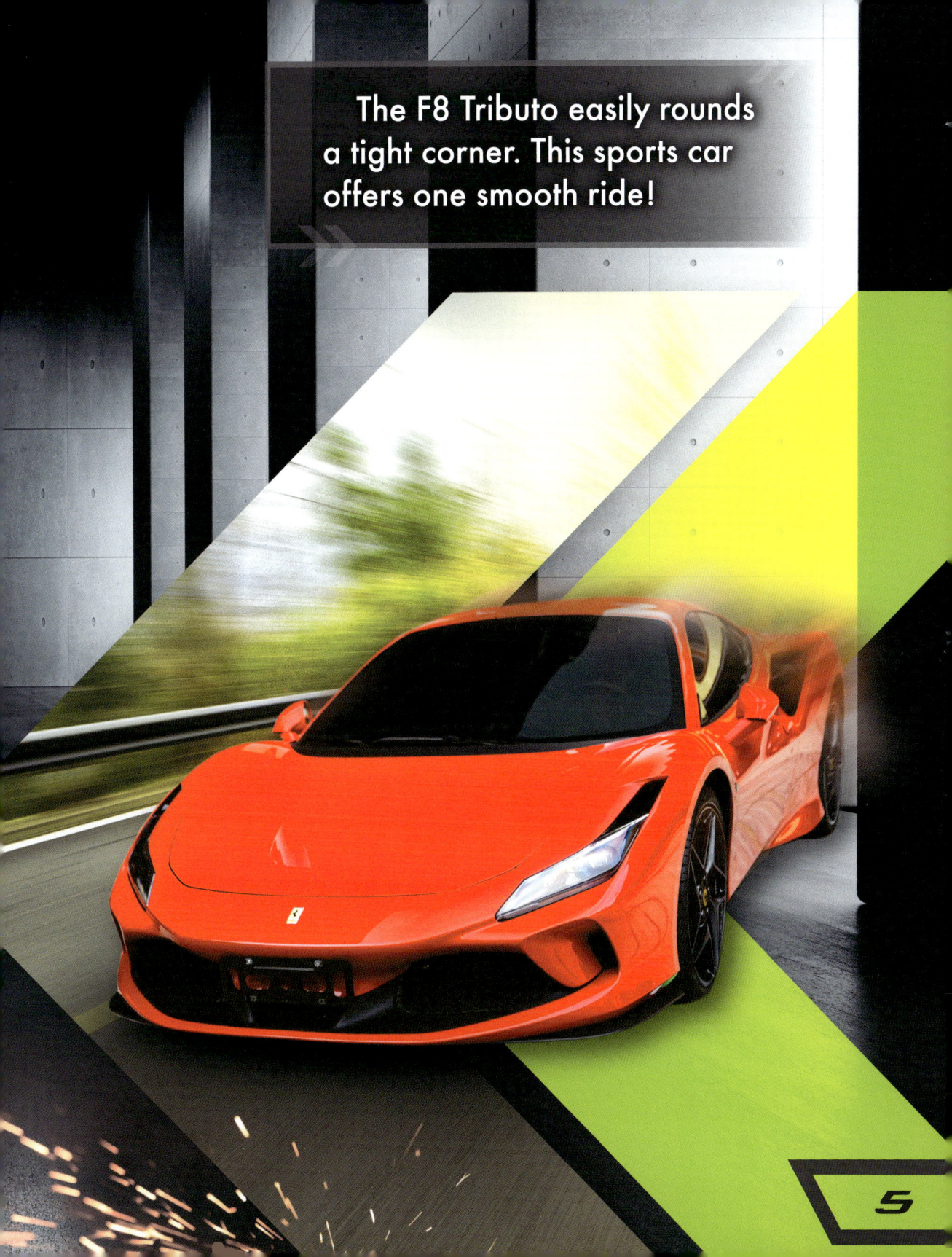
The F8 Tributo easily rounds a tight corner. This sports car offers one smooth ride!

ALL ABOUT THE F8 TRIBUTO »

FERRARI FACTORY IN MARANELLO, ITALY

Ferrari began in Maranello, Italy. The company's first car released in 1947. Its cars have won more than 5,000 races!

Ferraris are known for speed and **luxury**. Popular **models** include the 250 GTO, F40, and 812 Superfast.

BEHIND THE LOGO

Ferrari based its logo on one used by pilot Francesco Baracca. He painted a horse on his plane during World War I.

F40

WHERE IS IT MADE?

EUROPE

MARANELLO, ITALY

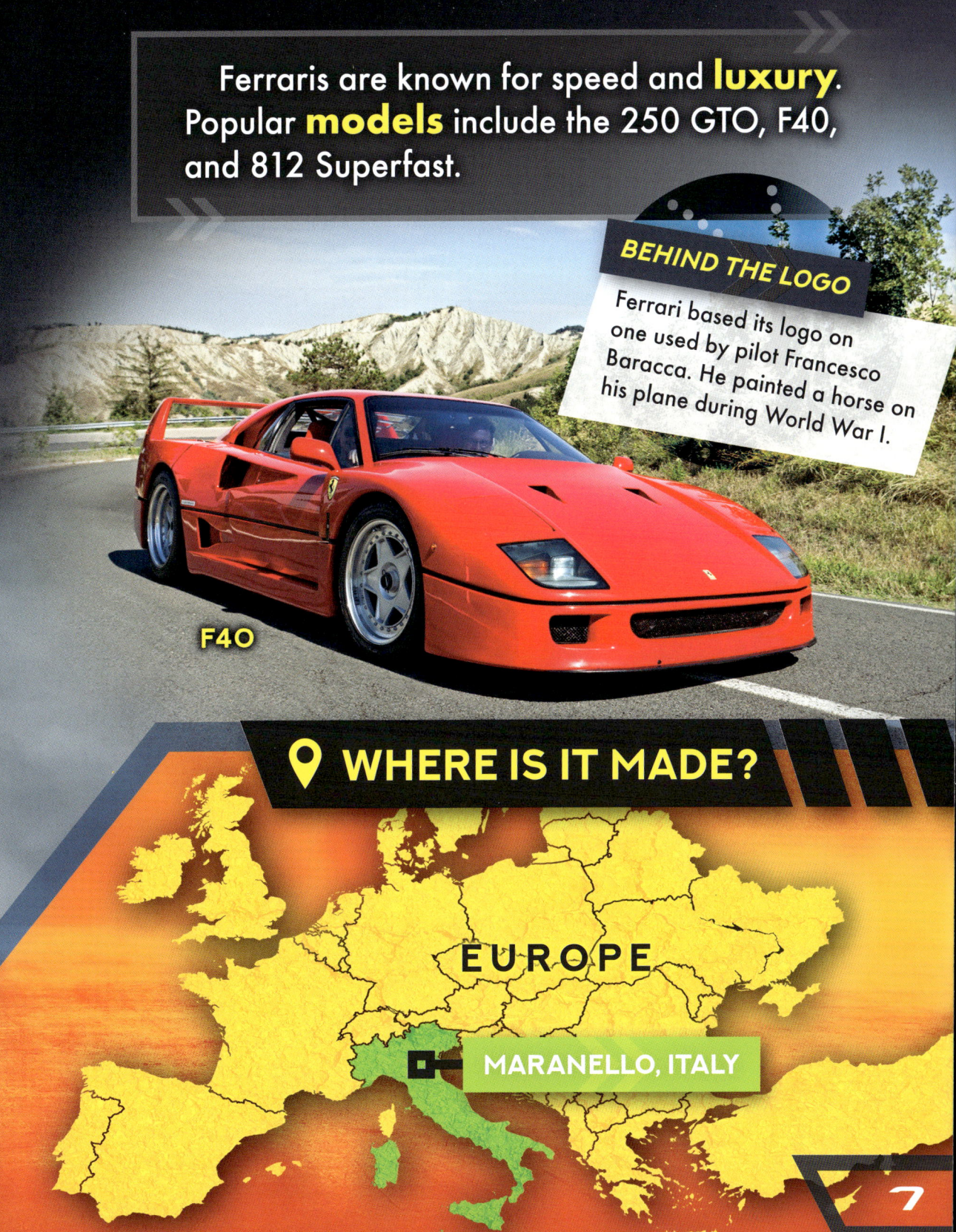

The Ferrari F8 Tributo **debuted** in 2019. It is an improved version of Ferrari's 488 model. The F8 Tributo is a **coupe**. Its **convertible** build is called the Spider.

F8 SPIDER

2019 F8 TRIBUTO

F8 TRIBUTO BASICS

YEAR FIRST MADE 2019

COST starts at $283,950

HOW MANY MADE more than 3,000

FEATURES

twin-turbo 3.9-liter V8 engine

S-duct

side splitters

The F8 Tributo's body is mostly **aluminum**. It is lighter than many Ferrari models. It was built to be fast.

The car reaches top speeds of 211 miles (340 kilometers) per hour!

PARTS OF THE F8 TRIBUTO

The F8 Tributo has Ferrari's most powerful **V8 engine** ever. It sends power to the rear wheels.

The car **accelerates** quickly. It reaches 60 miles (97 kilometers) per hour in just 2.9 seconds!

ENGINE SPECS

TWIN-TURBO 3.9-LITER V8

TOP SPEED — 211 miles (340 kilometers) per hour

0-60 TIME — 2.9 seconds

HORSEPOWER — 710 hp

The F8 Tributo sits low to the road. This gives the car great **handling**.

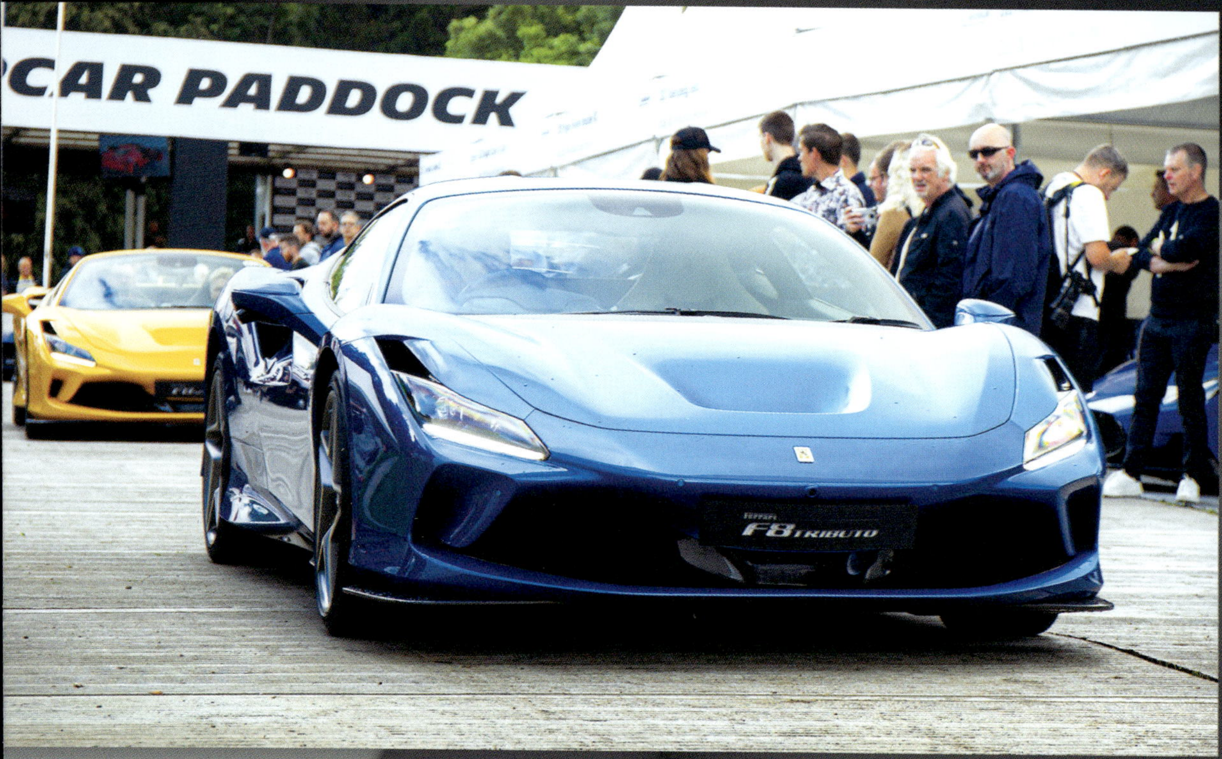
CAR PADDOCK
F8 TRIBUTO

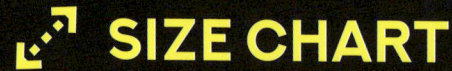

SIZE CHART

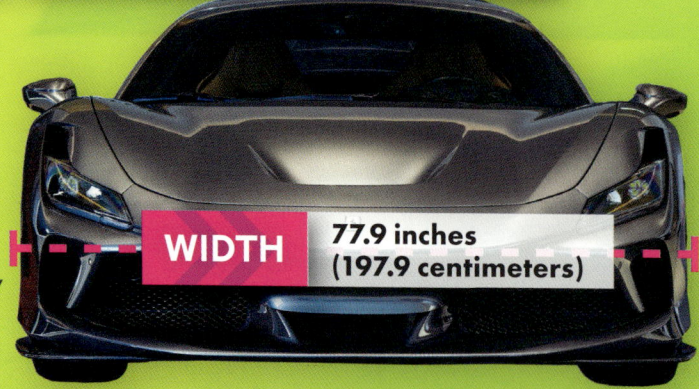

WIDTH
77.9 inches
(197.9 centimeters)

A wide **spoiler** sits on the back of the car. This helps the car stay on the road at high speeds.

SPOILER

HEIGHT 47.5 inches (120.7 centimeters)

LENGTH 181.5 inches (461 centimeters)

The Tributo has an **S-duct**. It sends air over the hood. This pushes the front down. It helps the car hold on to the road.

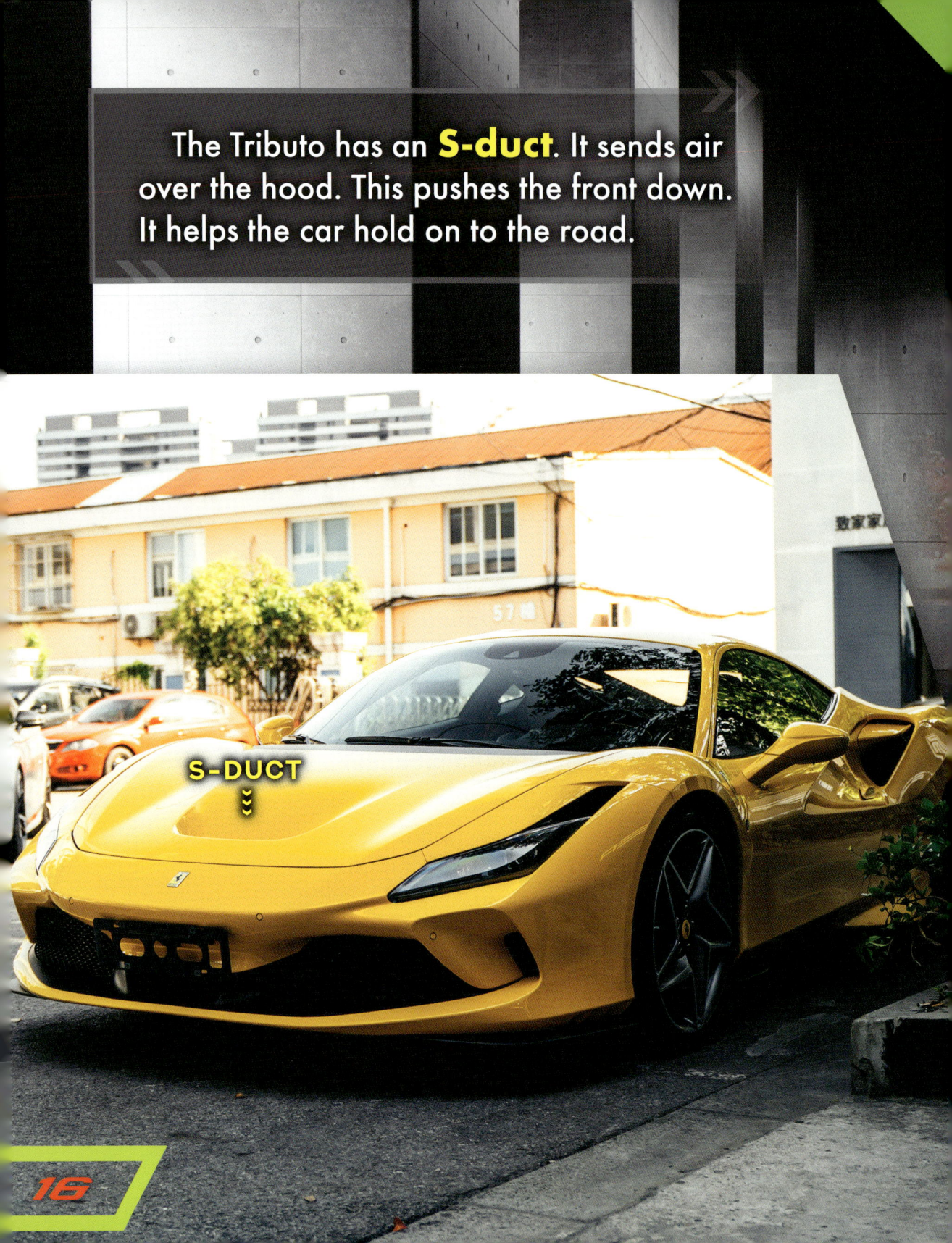

THE FASTEST ROLLER COASTER

The Formula Rossa is the world's fastest roller coaster. It was built by Ferrari. It speeds to 149 miles (240 kilometers) per hour!

LED TAILLIGHTS

TAILPIPE

The back of the car has two tailpipes. Four **LED** taillights sit under the spoiler.

STEERING WHEEL

The F8 Tributo has a flat-bottomed steering wheel. It is small in size. This makes for easy turns.

Drivers can choose from six seat options. They can also choose from 15 different inside colors.

RACING SEAT

A TRACK-READY FEEL
The F8 Tributo can come with racing seats!

THE F8 TRIBUTO'S FUTURE »

Ferrari stopped making the F8 Tributo in 2022. It introduced its first **SUV** in the same year. The company plans to release its first **electric car** in 2025.

The F8 Tributo is one of many cool Ferraris!

GLOSSARY

accelerates—increases in speed

aluminum—a strong, lightweight metal

convertible—a car with a folding or soft roof

coupe—a car with a hard roof and two doors

debuted—first came out

electric car—a car that does not need gas to run

handling—how a car performs around turns

LED—a type of light that saves energy and takes a very long time to burn out

luxury—a state of great pleasure or comfort

models—specific kinds of cars

S-duct—the part that controls airflow around a car to improve handling

spoiler—a part on the back of a car that helps the car grip the road

SUV—sport utility vehicle; an SUV is a type of car that often sits higher off the ground and can drive off road.

V8 engine—an engine with 8 cylinders arranged in the shape of a "V"

TO LEARN MORE

AT THE LIBRARY

Labrecque, Ellen. *Ferrari F8 Tributo*. Minneapolis, Minn.: Kaleidoscope, 2020.

Smith, Ryan. *Ferrari*. New York, N.Y.: AV2, 2021.

Sommer, Nathan. *Ferrari 812 Superfast*. Minneapolis, Minn.: Bellwether Media, 2022.

ON THE WEB

FACTSURFER

Factsurfer.com gives you a safe, fun way to find more information.

1. Go to www.factsurfer.com.

2. Enter "Ferrari F8 Tributo" into the search box and click 🔍.

3. Select your book cover to see a list of related content.

INDEX

Baracca, Francesco, 7
basics, 9
body, 10
colors, 19
company, 6, 7, 8, 12, 17, 20
convertible, 8
coupe, 8
electric car, 20
engine, 12, 13
engine specs, 12
Formula Rossa, 17
handling, 14
history, 6, 7, 8, 20
logo, 7
Maranello, Italy, 6, 7
models, 7, 8, 10
races, 6
S-duct, 16
seats, 19

size chart, 14–15
speed, 7, 10, 11, 12, 15, 17
Spider, 8
spoiler, 15, 17
steering wheel, 18
SUV, 20
taillights, 17
tailpipes, 17

The images in this book are reproduced through the courtesy of: unknown, front cover, p. 1; Grzegorz Czapski, pp. 3, 10-11 (left); Brandin Atchison/ Unsplash, p. 4; Jack Skeens, pp. 4-5, 14-15, 20-21 (right); D-VISIONS, p. 6; ermess, p. 7; VanderWolf Images, pp. 8-9; Lawrence Carmichael, p. 9 (isolated); classic topcar, pp. 9 (engine, s-duct), 12, 12-13, 14-15 (length), 16-17 (left), 18, 18-19; auto-data.net, p. 9 (splitter); dan74/ Alamy, pp. 10-11; Martyn Lucy/ Getty Images, p. 14; Artur_Nyk, p. 14; Hector Christiaen/ Alamy, pp. 16-17 (right); Everyonephoto Studio, pp. 20-21 (left).